My Secret Unicorn

Perfect Princesses

Kay Woodward
Illustrated by Strawberrie Donnelly

PUFFIN

PUFFIN BOOKS

Published by the Penguin Group
Penguin Books Ltd, 80 Strand, London WC2R 0RL, England
Penguin Group (USA) Inc., 375 Hudson Street, New York, New York 10014, USA
Penguin Group (Canada), 90 Eglinton Avenue East, Suite 700,
Toronto, Ontario, Canada M4P 2Y3
(a division of Pearson Penguin Canada Inc.)
Penguin Ireland, 25 St Stephen's Green, Dublin 2, Ireland (a division of Penguin Books Ltd)
Penguin Group (Australia), 250 Camberwell Road, Camberwell, Victoria 3124,
Australia (a division of Pearson Australia Group Pty Ltd)
Penguin Books India Pvt Ltd, 11 Community Centre, Panchsheel Park,
New Delhi – 110 017, India
Penguin Group (NZ), cnr Airborne and Rosedale Roads, Albany, Auckland 1310,
New Zealand (a division of Pearson New Zealand Ltd)
Penguin Books (South Africa) (Pty) Ltd, 24 Sturdee Avenue, Rosebank,
Johannesburg 2196, South Africa

Penguin Books Ltd, Registered Offices: 80 Strand, London WC2R 0RL, England

penguin.com

First published 2006

1

Text copyright © Kay Woodward, 2006
Illustrations copyright © Strawberrie Donnelly, 2006
All rights reserved

The moral right of the author and illustrator has been asserted

Set in Weiss

Made and printed in England by Clays Ltd, St Ives plc

Except in the United States of America, this book is sold subject to the condition
that it shall not, by way of trade or otherwise, be lent, re-sold, hired out, or
otherwise circulated without the publisher's prior consent in any form of binding
or cover other than that in which it is published and without a similar condition
including this condition being imposed on the subsequent purchaser

British Library Cataloguing in Publication Data
A CIP catalogue record for this book is available from the British Library

ISBN-13: 978–0–141–32084–7
ISBN-10: 0–141–32084–2

Contents

Welcome to the secret world of princesses... 1

Chapter One
All about princesses 3

Chapter Two
Fairy-tale princesses 8

Chapter Three
True-life princesses 13

Chapter Four
Castle life 18

Chapter Five
Princess duties 24

Chapter Six
Frocks, tiaras and trainers 30

Chapter Seven
The princess code of conduct 36

Chapter Eight
How to be a princess 42

Chapter Nine
How to spot a real princess 47

Chapter Ten
A perfect princess world 52

*Welcome to the secret world
of princesses . . .*

Have you ever wished you were a princess? Have you dreamed of riding in a golden coach and waving to crowds of cheering people? Would you like to live in the tallest turret tower of a fairy-tale castle?

Princesses are pretty, polite and perfect in every way. But there's much more to being a princess than meets the eye. How much do you really know about these royal girls?

Which musical instrument does a princess like to

play? What type of clothes would you find in her wardrobe? And how did she get to be a princess in the first place? Read on to find out more about the glittery, sparkly, twinkly and very, very secret world of princesses . . .

Chapter One
All about princesses

Princess Amanda awakes as soon as the first birds begin to chirrup. She gives a dainty yawn, stretches her arms high and then draws back the curtains surrounding her enormous bed. There is a gentle tap at the wooden door, which swings open to reveal her lady-in-waiting. She carries a tray laden with crunchy cereal, freshly squeezed apple juice and strawberries dipped in chocolate. Mmmm . . . This is a breakfast fit for a princess!

Princesses are incredibly lucky. Not only do they get to dress up in fancy outfits and wear sparkly tiaras – they're looked after and loved by lots of people too. So, if it's so fantastic, why isn't everyone a princess . . .?

Three of a kind

There are just three ways that a girl can become a royal princess . . .

Luck – any girl who is lucky enough to be the daughter or granddaughter of a king or queen is a princess. (Sleeping Beauty's parents were the king and queen.)

Love – marrying a prince is another way of becoming a princess. (This is how Cinderella got her royal tiara.)

Living in a very small country – some countries are so teeny that they don't have a king or queen. But they do have princes and princesses. However small the country, the rules are still the same – either you're born a princess or you marry a prince.

From past to present

Once upon a time, princesses lived in the highest towers of turreted castles. They went to huge banquets and feasted on pheasant and swan. Each princess had a maid whose job was to brush the princess's long hair a thousand times every morning and evening.

Modern princesses are much busier than princesses from olden times, but some things remain the same. Princesses still live in castles or palaces. And they still dress up in glittering gowns to attend splendid royal banquets and spectacular balls.

To be a queen

One day, when she is quite grown up, a princess may become a queen. This happens when the old king and queen die, or when they decide that they are too old to be in charge any more.

Not very long ago, the eldest prince was always next in line to the throne. Even if he had an older sister, the prince would leapfrog his way to the royal hot seat. This was very unfair on princesses. Only princesses who didn't have any brothers had a real chance of becoming queen. But now things have changed. In the twenty-first century, the eldest child of a king or queen is usually the next monarch – whether they are a prince or a princess. Hurrah!

Perfect princess facts

The daughter of an emperor or empress is also called a princess.

It was once said that a princess is born with a silver spoon in her mouth. This is, of course, ridiculous! However, it is traditional to feed baby princesses from solid silver spoons. If silver spoons aren't available, gold will do. But never plastic.

Princesses are often given heaps of names – Princess Beatrice, from the British royal family, is officially known as Her Royal Highness Beatrice Elizabeth Mary of York. What a mouthful!

Chapter Two
Fairy-tale princesses

Rapunzel's fingers move so quickly they are a blur. She takes one flaxen handful of hair from the right, then the left, then the right . . . until she has a plait that is longer than any rope. She gazes from the window of her tower prison. Tonight, she will let down her hair once more, but the wicked witch will not climb up Rapunzel's long, long plait. This time, it will be the handsome prince. He is coming to rescue her.

Much of what people know about princesses comes from fairy tales. Without Rapunzel, who would know that princesses plait their hair?

Without Cinderella, who would know that princesses have small feet? And without peas, who would be able to recognize a real princess in the first place . . .?

The princess and the pea

Once upon a time, there was a handsome prince named Robert, who desperately wanted to marry a real princess. He'd met hundreds of princesses, but none of them were quite right. Some couldn't curtsy, and some didn't know how to dance. One princess couldn't even balance a tiara upon her head!

Then, one night, there was a terrible storm. Lightning flashed, thunder growled and a fierce wind whipped around the royal castle. The prince slept soundly, but his mother – Queen

Marion – heard a loud knocking. Outside was a cold, tired girl, wearing a ragged dress. The girl said she was a princess. But the queen wasn't so sure – although she did know a way to find out.

That night, the queen made up a bed for the ragged girl. First, she placed a pea on the bed. Then she piled twenty mattresses and twenty blankets on top. The bed was so high that the girl needed a stepladder to climb on to it.

In the morning, the queen asked the visitor if she'd slept well. 'Not at all,' the girl replied. She'd been so uncomfortable and she'd tossed and turned all night. At this, the queen knew that the girl – her name was Linda – really was a princess. Only a princess would have felt a pea through so many mattresses and blankets. Queen Marion told her son, who was delighted. And Prince Robert and Princess Linda lived happily ever after.

The most important guests of all

Everyone who's ever heard the story of Sleeping Beauty will know that godmothers are very important people – especially to a princess. When a princess is just a baby, her godmothers promise to take special care of her. As the princess grows up, they will protect her from wicked witches and broken bones. They'll try extra hard to keep her safe from the sharpest spinning-wheel needle. In return, all they want is the princess's happiness.

However, it is worth remembering that godmothers can sometimes become a little cross if they don't receive an invitation to a royal birthday party. (They simply adore parties.) So, if you are a princess and you have a birthday soon, check your guest list carefully. You wouldn't want to forget to invite your godmothers . . .

Perfect princess facts

❀ *Cinderella had such small feet that she usually wore children's shoes. With feet this small, it's no wonder that there was no other woman in the entire kingdom who could squeeze her toes into Cinderella's glass slipper!*

❀ *Danish author Hans Christian Andersen wrote over 200 stories and fairy tales for children. Some of his most famous tales were* The Princess and the Pea, Thumbelina *and* The Snow Queen.

❀ *Fairy-tale princesses do not always kiss handsome princes. They have been known to kiss frogs and beasts too. Look out for* The Frog Prince *and* Beauty and the Beast.

Chapter Three
True-life princesses

The girl closes her storybook and lays it gently on the bedside table. She loves reading about fairy-tale princesses, especially the happy endings. She lies back against the silken pillows and thinks about how lucky she is ... She doesn't have a wicked stepmother, or a bad fairy godmother. And she isn't forced to work in a cellar. Yes, it's much better to be a real princess than a fairy-tale one. The princess smiles and goes to sleep.

Many years ago, there was an unwritten royal rule: princes had to marry princesses. (Of course, there were a few royals who broke this rule —

remember how Prince
Charming married
lucky old Cinders?)
Sometimes, they
married because
they'd fallen in love.
But sometimes, a prince
married a princess because their
two countries wanted to make friends. Now, the
royal rule is history. Princes and princesses can
marry anyone they like! Here are some true
stories of princess brides...

The film-star princess

There was once a beautiful American actress
called Grace Kelly. During the 1950s, she
starred in lots of Hollywood films, including
High Noon, *Rear Window*, *To Catch a Thief* and
High Society. And then she met a prince. Prince
Rainier was the head of the royal family in
Monaco – a tiny kingdom in the south of France.

In 1956, after a whirlwind romance, the film star and the prince were married. Princess Grace of Monaco took up her new royal duties at once and never returned to acting. But she is still remembered for her wonderful films. Look out for them on rainy Saturday afternoons – they're smashing!

The newsreader princess

Letizia Ortiz was a famous – and award-winning – Spanish newsreader long before she became a princess. Then, in 2002, she travelled to the north-west coast of Spain to report the story of a tanker that had spilled tonnes of oil into the sea. It was an environmental disaster. Prince Felipe came to offer his support – and met Letizia. The couple saw each other secretly for a whole year, as they didn't want their romance to be splashed all over the newspapers. But then the royal engagement was announced and Letizia and Felipe married in Madrid in May 2004. One day, the ex-newsreader will be the Queen of Spain.

The businesswoman princess

Top Australian businesswoman Mary Donaldson never dreamed that her next job would be as a princess. In 2000, she met a handsome young man called Fred and liked him straight away. What she didn't know was that Fred was actually Crown Prince Frederik of Denmark. When they decided to get married, Mary had to make lots of changes to her life. She became a Danish citizen, changed her religion and learned to speak fluent Danish. But when she walked down the aisle in May 2004, Crown Princess Mary of Denmark didn't forget her own country. She carried a bouquet of Danish and Australian flowers.

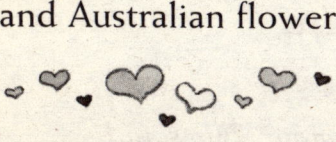

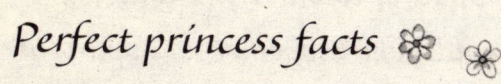

Perfect princess facts

❀ *A crown princess is not a princess who wears a crown all the time. She is a princess who will one day be a queen or empress.*

❀ *Diana, Princess of Wales, was president or patron of over a hundred different charities. She was particularly fond of supporting children's and homeless people's charities.*

❀ *Being a princess or a prince is a full-time job. There are lots of official duties to carry out. That's why princesses and princes don't have time to do normal jobs as well.*

Chapter Four
Castle life

The ballroom is a blur of colour. Blues and greens, reds and golds whirl together and apart, in time to the magical music. Princess Mia gazes at the dancers, wishing that she were old enough to join in. She knows all the steps, after all. Then her father approaches, bows and holds out his arm. The princess springs to her feet at once, then curtsies politely. The princess and the king begin to dance.

One of the coolest things about being a princess is living in a castle. It's packed with mysterious nooks and crannies, winding staircases and gloomy dungeons.

There's a ballroom, a banqueting hall and picture galleries lined with works of art and heaps more fascinating places to explore and huge rooms to relax in. But they weren't always like this . . .

In the olden days . . .

Hundreds of years ago, you had to be really tough to live in a castle. They weren't nearly as cosy and warm as they are today. Windows were just holes in the wall — there was no glass in them. Heavy drapes helped to keep out the cold, but castles were still very draughty places. There were no carpets either — the floors were covered with straw. And central heating was out of the question. (Although they did have lovely, roasty-toasty fires.)

But nothing was as bad as the princess's bathroom. There was no fluffy bathmat, no posh bidet, no scented hand wash, no frothy bubble bath and no quilted toilet paper. Worst of all, the toilet emptied straight into the moat. Eeewww!

The princess's chamber

Once glass had been slotted into windows and thick, luxurious rugs rolled over the floors, castles instantly became much more comfortable places to live. And the best rooms of all were the royal quarters. A princess's chamber was often right at the top of a tower, so the walls were curved. Inside, it was sparkling and sumptuous beyond belief. The walls were hung with tapestries and silk banners. There was a huge four-poster bed, piled high with embroidered quilts and soft cushions. At night, curtains all round the bed were pulled shut so that the princess was extra snug.

Royal feasts

On special occasions, royal families invite all their best friends, fellow kings and queens and other important people to the castle for a banquet. The guests – sometimes well over a hundred of them – sit at a really long table, where they are served with all sorts of tasty treats.

Long ago, chefs roasted pigs, cows and swans – yes, really! – for a royal banquet. This was because rich people liked a lot of meat in the olden days. They didn't realize that vegetables were good for them. Now, a mouth-watering menu includes fish, meat, tasty veg, salad and a posh pudding. Sometimes, delicate gold leaf is dabbed on to tarts and trifles so that they sparkle and shine.

After the meal, it's time for the real fun to start. The royal family leads the way into the ballroom, where the musicians are waiting. It's time for the princess to dance wonderful waltzes and terrific tangos with anyone she chooses!

Perfect princess facts

❀ When a banquet is held at Windsor Castle, near London, even the tiniest things are given the royal treatment. Someone even shapes the butter into small pats and stamps each one with a crown!

❀ At royal banquets, one of the butlers uses a ruler to check that all plates, glasses, knives, forks and spoons are exactly the same distance apart.

❀ Before televisions and DVDs were invented, royal families used to listen to live music for entertainment. Minstrels (musicians, not chocolatey treats) played on flutes and trumpets, bagpipes and guitars. Princesses learned to play instruments too – their number-one choice was the harp.

Chapter Five
Princess duties

Princess Leilani flips open her diary to check what's happening today. Hmm, it looks like it's going to be busy. First, she's visiting an old people's home . . . then she's off to open a new road . . . then she's presenting an award for bravery. And that's only the morning! The princess takes a deep breath. She knows what she must do. She brandishes her toothbrush, then twists the top off the toothpaste tube. She's going to do a great deal of smiling today — she'd better make sure that her teeth are sparkly clean!

Being a princess isn't all fun and games — there's work to do too. Like other members of a royal family, princesses are responsible for representing their country and for carrying out official duties.

Behind the curtain

Every time a princess declares a building officially open, she tugs a golden cord, which sweeps back a tiny velvet curtain. And behind that curtain is a plaque with lots of important information on it. In the future, people can read the plaque to find out about the day that the building was opened . . .

The Museum of Very Arty Things
was officially opened on 18 August
by Princess Jill of Barrovia.

Think of how many times you've pulled your bedroom curtains open — then multiply that number by ten. This figure might be somewhere near the average number of times a princess pulls back curtains in her lifetime!

Princesses and pop stars

A princess is a little like a pop star. Both are famous. They both dress up in sparkly outfits and appear in front of crowds of people. And they both love to do good deeds. But pop stars and princesses raise money for charity in totally different ways.

Pop stars record smash-hit songs that sell thousands of copies and raise heaps of cash. Princesses don't — and there's a very good reason for this. (They may have many talents, but singing is usually not one of them. Most princesses are better at other things – they cannot sing. They have truly dreadful singing voices.) So instead of deafening everyone, they make sure that different charities get lots and lots of publicity instead.

No rest for a princess

During term time, younger princesses go to lessons like other girls of their age. They don't have much time for royal duties. But in the holidays – when everyone else is reading, riding bikes or jumping around in sparkling swimming pools – princesses go to work!

During a single day, a princess might open a library, visit sick children in hospital, munch through a posh lunch (princesses are rarely allowed to eat burgers), watch a gymnastics display, plant a tree, go to a film premiere and shake 500 hands. Phew! Wouldn't you rather read a book . . .?

Perfect princess facts

If the king and queen are busy, princesses have to knight people. (They do this by gently placing a sword on each of a man's shoulders, which turns him into a royal knight.) They use a light sword that is easy to handle. (After all, they wouldn't want to accidentally chop someone's head off!)

❀ Some lucky princesses are ambidextrous. This means that they can write with either hand. (Handy, eh?) It also means that they can shake hands with their left or their right hand, so their hands only get half as tired.

❀ Princesses are in real demand. So if you ever want a princess to open a school fête or to come to your birthday party, be sure to ask her with plenty of time to spare — princesses get booked up years in advance!

Chapter Six
Frocks, tiaras and trainers

Princess Donna gazes at the mirror. She hardly recognizes the girl in the reflection. Where has the ordinary-looking girl in the school uniform gone? This girl is wearing a dress of shimmering turquoise silk. Round her waist is a sash of pure white. Jewels sparkle at her throat, and on her head is a twinkling tiara. She smiles. And the princess smiles back.

Princesses love to dress up in big, flouncy frocks as much as the next girl – but even they would get tired of wearing ball gowns every day of the week. Instead, their wardrobes are packed with row upon row of dresses, suits, hats and shoes of every colour. Whatever they do — walking, dancing, horse-riding or archery — princesses always have the perfect outfit for every occasion.

Inside the royal wardrobe

If you ever had the chance to step inside a princess's wardrobe — which is usually an entire room instead of a single cupboard — you would be amazed with a capital A. Here are just some of the extra-special things you might find there . . .

Posh gowns — princesses have lots of posh dresses made of satin and silk and taffeta and lace. They have long dresses, short dresses, dresses with pointy sleeves and dresses so big that they could hide a whole class of children beneath the skirt.

Twinkly tiaras – royal crowns can be pretty heavy (each one weighs as much as a bag of sugar), so to make sure that a princess's slender neck doesn't ache she often wears a tiara instead. A tiara is much lighter, but just as twinkly as a crown, and it won't fall off during a lively dance.

Flowing cloaks – a hoodie or a denim jacket just doesn't look right with a ball gown, but a flowing cloak will hang neatly over a frilly frock without squishing it. A princess will usually have a couple of these – a cool silk cloak for summer and a thick velvet one for winter.

Silk sashes – these are essential princess-wear. A sash can be wrapped round a party dress or draped from shoulder to waist for a posh dinner do.

Sparkly shoes – a princess can never have too many pairs of shoes. She has pink shoes, blue shoes, silver shoes, and gold shoes and even sporty trainers – all with a generous sprinkling of sparkles.

Shiny trinkets – the royal jewels are locked away in a safe, but princesses keep a few favourite beads and trinkets handy, in case they need to dress up in a hurry.

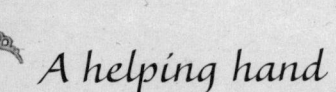

A helping hand

Imagine wearing one outfit in the morning, another in the afternoon and a totally different set of clothes in the evening... This is what princesses often do. After all, they couldn't wear the same set of clothes to a hospital, then a polo match, followed by an awards ceremony.

This is where the lady's maid comes in — it's her job to look after the princess and her wardrobe. She washes, irons and mends the princess's clothes, so that they are in tippity-top condition. And, when there are lots of buttons, belts and zips to sort out, she helps the princess to get dressed and undressed too.

Perfect princess facts

❀ A princess is far too busy to go around Miss Selfridge and New Look on a Saturday. Instead, she hosts her own private fashion shows back at the castle.

❀ A princess doesn't like to be caught wearing the same dress as someone else. Often, fashion designers will make just one copy of an evening gown to make sure that the princess is the only person in the whole world to be wearing it.

❀ Princesses have their very own pair of glass slippers, just like Cinderella. These are crafted by a master glassblower, who makes sure that the slippers fit their owner — and no one else — perfectly.

Chapter Seven
The princess code of conduct

The royal carriage rolls through the palace gates, between the crowded pavements. A small face peers anxiously out of the window. It's the princess, and she's on her way to her first royal engagement. She'll have to curtsy to countless kings and queens – without tripping up – and speak politely to everyone she meets. She takes a deep breath and holds up a trembling hand at the carriage window. Slowly, she begins to wave – and the crowd cheers!

There's no doubt about it – you won't meet a politer person than a princess. They know everything there is to know about manners, from the proper way to walk and curtsy to the correct fork to use for eating fish.

Princess footsteps

A princess might know perfectly well how to walk – and run and jump and hop and skip – but she has to learn to walk in a royal way too. Here's how to do a royal walk . . .

1. Look for the biggest hardback book on your shelf – a dictionary or a book of fairy tales is ideal.
2. Choose the biggest room in your house and clear a path across the middle of it.
3. Now, pull your shoulders back and stand up really straight. (You could pretend that you have an invisible string attached to the top of your head that is pulling you up, up, upwards.)
4. Balance the book carefully on top of your head, then hang your arms by your sides.
5. Walk slowly across the room without letting

the book fall off your head.
(Don't touch the book —
that's cheating!)

After some practice, it
should become much easier
to walk without the book
tumbling to the floor. You
will find that you're moving
very smoothly, almost as if
you are gliding. Now, take
the book off your head and walk across the
room again. Ta-daaaa! You're walking just like
a princess!

Princess speak
When a princess speaks, it might sound like a
foreign language, but she's just using extra-polite
words. Here are some common princess-like
phrases:

I'm very pleased to meet you.   Hi!

How do you do?   Are you OK?

Thank you kindly.   Ta.

Would you mind awfully if I . . .?   Can I . . .?

Do excuse me.   Whoops! Pardon me.

Could I have your attention, please?   Oi! You, over there!

I'm very pleased to meet you

How to curtsy

A curtsy is the special bend-down-stand-up movement that girls and women do to show respect when they meet a royal person. Even princesses curtsy to kings and queens. A curtsy is meant to be slow and graceful, so take your time – don't rush it.

1. Step to the left with your left foot, with your toes pointing outwards. At the same time, swing your arms out to the side.
2. Slide your right foot behind the left, with those toes pointing outwards too.
3. Bend both knees and lower your body slowly, while bowing your head to the floor to look at your feet.
4. If you're wearing a long princess dress, you can make the curtsy look extra-special by holding on to the side seams of your skirt.

A curtsy can be performed to the right too. Simply swap left for right and right for left in the above instructions.

Perfect princess facts

❀ Princesses learn to say 'Hello' and 'How are you?' and 'Goodbye' in lots of different languages. This means that when they visit foreign countries they can always speak to the people they meet, even if it's just a few words.

❀ At banquets and posh dinner parties, each person has a whole row of cutlery. So which knives and forks do you use first? It's easy — simply start with the cutlery furthest from your plate and work your way inwards.

❀ Did you know that there is supposed to be a correct way to tilt a bowl of soup? Princesses always tilt the bowl away from them before scooping up the last spoonfuls. Try this with your breakfast cereal, but be warned . . . it isn't easy!

Chapter Eight
How to be a princess

Princess Pippa leans back against the helicopter seat and closes her eyes. She has done so much handshaking and so much royal waving today that her arm feels like it's made of jelly. Then she thinks of the bubble bath that awaits her at the castle. And the crown-shaped pizza and yummy chocolate tart that she'll eat afterwards. She gives a royal smile as the helicopter swoops downwards.

You don't have to be born in a castle to be a princess — anyone can be a princess if they try. After you've learned the princess code of conduct (see page 36), try the top royal tips in this chapter. You'll soon be the coolest princess ever!

Get the princess look

If you're going to be a princess, the first thing to do is to look like one. First, find the poshest outfit in your wardrobe – a party dress is perfect. And how about some accessories? Do you have a sparkly cardigan or a sequinned belt? You'll need some princess shoes too. A pair of ballet pumps will look really royal.

Once you've finished your outfit, how about your hair? If you have long locks, plait them like Rapunzel, or ask a friend to pin your hair up.

If your hair is short, add a couple of sparkly slides. Then it's time for the finishing touch – a tiara. If you have spare birthday money, you could treat yourself to a tiara from an accessory shop. Or, better still, make your own (see page 52). And don't forget to paint your nails when you're done!

Champion handshakers

The number of times that a princess shakes hands during a single day can be astronomical! That's why, at the end of a very busy day, you might find a princess relaxing in front of the television with one hand in a bowl of icy-cold water. To make sure that handshaking doesn't give you the shakes, follow these three simple rules:

1. Grasp the other person's hand firmly, but not too tight.
2. Give just one shake – otherwise, it will take you hours to meet and greet a whole room of people.
3. If you meet a good friend, give them a quick kiss on the cheek instead!

A really royal title

Princesses don't have surnames. Instead, they have special titles to show where they are from or the country which they rule. For example, they might be called Princess Lisa of Wales or Princess Dereen of Leicestershire. Why not make up your very own title or create a pretty coat of arms? You're guaranteed to feel as royal as a real princess!

Perfect princess facts

❀ Reading fairy tales will help you to get into a proper princessy mood. Not only are they packed with vital princess information, they're really good stories too.

❀ On average, a princess has to smile 1,440 times a day — that's a lot of smiling. So, if you're going to be a princess, you'll have to practise smiling too. Otherwise, you could end up with a really achy face every evening.

❀ Why not keep your own make-believe princess diary? You could write about the wonderful places you'd like to go to and the brilliant things you'd like to do. And, one day, they might come true . . .

Chapter Nine
How to spot a real princess

Rose swings gently to and fro beneath the great oak tree. In the distance, she spies a horse galloping swiftly towards her. Within minutes, the horse skids to a halt in front of the swing. A messenger dismounts, unfurls a long scroll and begins to read: 'The king wishes to inform you that you are his long-lost granddaughter. Technically speaking, this makes you a princess. From now on, you will be known as Princess Rose.'

He jumps on his horse and rides away. Rose stares after him in amazement. A princess? Really? Finally, her dream has come true! She is a princess!

You might not realize it, but perhaps your great-great-great-great-great-great-great-great-great granddad was a king, which would make YOU a princess. But how do you find out for sure? Here are some tried and tested ways to check if you or your friends have royal blood.

The perfect princess test

To find out whether you could be a perfect princess, answer the following questions truthfully. You'll need a sheet of paper and a pencil to write down the answers. And you'll also need a watch or a clock to time yourself for question numbers 9 and 10. Are you ready? Good luck! Go!

1. Do you always say please, thank you and excuse me?
2. Do you enjoy soaking in a bath sprinkled with rose petals?
3. Are you kind to others?

4. Does a tiara fit on top of your head really well?
5. Can you perform a royal wave?
6. How about a curtsy?
7. Do you like the story of Cinderella more than Puss in Boots?
8. Do you know how to plait hair?
9. Can you talk for one full minute about why you would be a perfect princess?
10. Can you smile non-stop for twenty minutes?

If you said YES to nine or more of the questions, there's a big chance that you might be a princess. At the very least, you're a highly princessy person.

The pea test

There are only two ways of finding out for certain whether someone is a real princess or not. For one princess test, a pea has to be placed under a huge pile of mattresses and duvets (see page 9), but this is difficult to arrange if you don't live in a castle. The second test is the pillow test . . .

The pillow test

Gather together a cotton handkerchief, a pretty flower, a stick of cinnamon and a bunch of fresh mint leaves. Carefully wrap the flower, cinnamon and mint in the handkerchief and place the fragrant bundle under your pillow. Go to bed as usual. If you dream of a royal coronation, where a crown is placed upon your head, then the answer is simple: one day, you really will be a princess!

Perfect princess facts

❀ Real princesses are very good at playing musical instruments.

❀ They are especially talented harpists, but are expert at playing the recorder too. Can you play the recorder . . .?

❀ The top ten favourite princess names of all time are: Emily, Ellie, Jessica, Sophie, Victoria, Chloe, Lucy, Elizabeth, Olivia, Charlotte, Katie and Megan. Do you have a name fit for a princess?

❀ A real princess has a very good sense of smell. She can smell baking bread and melting chocolate from over a kilometre away!

Chapter Ten
A perfect princess world

*I*f you'd love to be a princess, why not make these royal accessories for yourself and your room? Then you can make believe that you too are a perfect princess!

A glittering tiara
Every princess should have her own tiara – the sparklier the better! Here's what you need to make yours . . .

💚 A piece of stiff card
💚 A sheet of tracing paper
💚 A pencil

- A pair of scissors
- Silver paint
- Glue
- Multicoloured sequins
- A plastic Alice band
- Sticky tape

1. Make a cardboard shape following the outline on the next page. You can do this by tracing the image on to tracing paper and flipping the paper over. Then, pressing firmly with a pencil, rub this outline on to a piece of card. Cut out the card shape.

2. Paint the cardboard shape carefully and wait until it is totally dry.

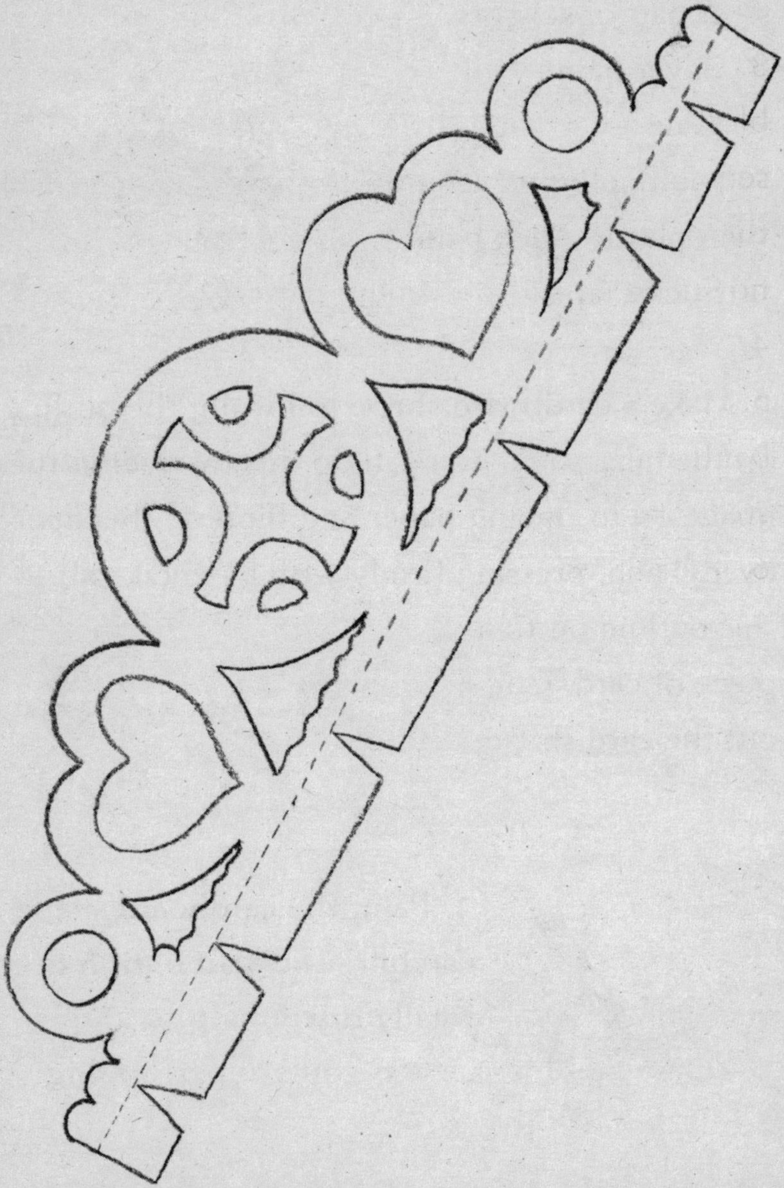

3. Using very small blobs of glue, stick the sequins to the front of the silver tiara. Why not create your own sequin pattern?

4. Wait until the glue is dry.

5. Fold the tiara tabs underneath the Alice band and then stick the tiara to the band with sticky tape.

6. Your tiara is now ready to wear!

Top tip: use a couple of hair clips to secure the tabs to your hair. This will help to stop the tiara wobbling when you are performing royal duties.

Really royal drapes

Princesses usually sleep in four-poster beds, but it might be difficult to fit one of these into your bedroom. And, whether you sleep in a bed or a bunk, these beautiful drapes will make your slumber zone look extra special. Here's what you need . . .

♡ A piece of netting or silky material (about 1 metre wide and 3 metres long)
♡ A hook
♡ A large curtain ring
♡ Sequins, sparkles and glittery bits

1. Ask your mum and dad to screw a hook into the wall about a metre above the headboard of your bed.

2. Decorate the material with as many sparkly things as you can find.

3. Then thread the material through the curtain ring until the ring is in the middle. Knot the material, so it stays in the same place, knotted to the ring.

4. Hang the curtain ring on the hook and then – in an arty way – drape the two ends of the material either side of your bed.

5. Lie on your bed and admire your handiwork. Do you feel like a princess now . . .?

A jewellery box fit for a princess

Do you have somewhere special to keep beautiful beads and twinkly tiaras? No? Well, don't worry – this jewellery box is easy to make and looks terrific. Here's what you'll need . . .

- ♥ A shoebox
- ♥ Glue
- ♥ A piece of velvet (60 cm x 45 cm)
- ♥ A pair of scissors
- ♥ A stapler
- ♥ A sheet of pretty wrapping paper
- ♥ Sticky tape

1. Blob glue all over the inside of the shoebox.
2. Lay the velvet inside the box with the furry, velvety side upwards. Rub your hands over the material to make sure that it's stuck firmly. (It doesn't matter if the velvet wrinkles – this will look extra posh.)

3. Carefully trim off the velvet at the top of the box until there is about 2 cm hanging over each edge.
4. Now staple all round the top of the shoebox to keep the velvet in position. (The long, smooth parts of the staples should be inside the box.)

5. Cover the outside of the shoebox with wrapping paper, sticking it in position with glue and sticky tape. The paper should go right to the top of the box edges, covering the velvety edges.

6. Finally, cover the shoebox lid with wrapping paper. Ta-daaaa! Now all that's left to do is fill your jewellery box with all your special bits and bobs. There might even be enough room to pop this book inside . . .